Edward Everett Hale

Everyday sermons

Edward Everett Hale

Everyday sermons

ISBN/EAN: 9783743349742

Manufactured in Europe, USA, Canada, Australia, Japa

Cover: Foto ©ninafisch / pixelio.de

Manufactured and distributed by brebook publishing software (www.brebook.com)

Edward Everett Hale

Everyday sermons

EVERY-DAY SERMONS.

BY

EDWARD E. HALE, D.D.,
Minister South Congregational Church, Boston.

"Teaching them to observe all things whatsoever I have commanded you; and, lo, I am with you alway, even unto the end of the world."
MATT. xxviii. 20.

BOSTON:
J. STILMAN SMITH & CO.,
3 HAMILTON PLACE.
1892.

CONTENTS.

	PAGE
THE WORTH OF ENTHUSIASM	3
WHAT THINK YE OF CHRIST?	17
FIVE QUESTIONS	31
FATHER, SON, AND HOLY SPIRIT	45
HOW IMMORTALS LIVE	59
IMITATORS OF GOD	71
INSTALLATION OF REV. JOHN CUCKSON	83

THE WORTH OF ENTHUSIASM.

"I have given you authority to tread upon serpents and scorpions, and over all the power of the enemy; and nothing shall by any means hurt you." — LUKE x. 19.

It is a vivid statement, in prophetic symbolism, of the sway of their enthusiasm over the obstacles which were to come before them. The history of those centuries more than makes good the prophecy. These people, forgetting themselves, and determined to bring in the kingdom of God, went forward, conquering and to conquer; and it was as he said, — the annoying serpents and scorpions, who are in the pathway of such travellers, should not hinder them so but that they should succeed. If you talk to-day to any low-toned person who has been in the West Indies, he will tell you of the abomination of the scorpions who perhaps stray upon your pillows, and of the terror of the serpents who infest the forests. But for all that, when the Spanish race landed there, determined to find gold, they went forward to success, — they trod upon the serpents and the scorpions, and they do not so much as appear in their history.

Here, then, is Christ's statement of the aggressive power of Christian enthusiasm. It is a statement made in advance, and we may make a like statement as we look backward upon the course of history. Just at this moment the English-speaking world is called upon to ask whether it believes that this statement is still true, or whether the more mechanical processes of the nineteenth century have gained such control of society that we can no longer rely upon it. The square statement which General Booth makes, in this remarkable book of his, "In Darkest England," is that he and his are able to tread on the serpents and scorpions which have deterred other people in their efforts to clean up the dark places of London, and to bring in the light of a decent civilization in their place. To this the Archbishop of Canterbury and Mr. Huxley and the people, whom I may call the regulation philanthropists, reply that it is quite impossible. They say that there are a great many serpents in the way, and a great many very annoying scorpions in the way. They tell how large the scorpions are, — they have measured some of them. And they tell how bad the bite of the serpents is, and they say that, with such obstacles in the way, it is idle to undertake to relieve these difficulties. They say the serpents must be killed and the scorpions stifled first; and yet they do not show any method of killing the serpents or of stifling the scorpions. It is quite as in the Book of Proverbs it is said that the sluggard says, there is a lion in the path. Not that it is fair to say that the Archbishop of Canterbury or Mr. Huxley are either of them indolent men. But it is quite fair to say that the lions which they see out of their windows, or think they see, are so hungry and noisy that they dare not leave palace or college to go out to attack them.

General Booth does. General Booth says that he has an army of fanatics at his disposal, who will do what he tells them to do, and that the enthusiasm of their Christian faith is so great that it will enable them to overcome the inconveniences which they find in their way. He does not use the particular figure which the Saviour uses, of serpents and scorpions. He knows that the nineteenth century prefers to have square statements of the visible fact. It does not like this form of Oriental imagery, and it considers it quite out of the way. So he devotes himself, with more or less statistical statement, such as the nineteenth century does like, to show how he can take the tramps who have gathered together in the worst regions of London; how he can embody them under a certain military form; how he can march them into the country, and place them on farms which we should think ridiculously small; how he can set them upon market-gardening; or, at the least, how every man with a spade can earn his own ration. This, at bottom, is the plan for darkest England which General Booth proposes. And for this plan he is now engaged in collecting five hundred thousand dollars as a capital stock, and an annual income of one hundred fifty thousand dollars to carry it forward, till, in its success, it shall support itself. I have not observed that he once speaks of it as an experiment. He speaks with the definiteness with which the Saviour of men himself speaks. He says that they have divine power with them, that they will tread on all the serpents, that they will stifle all the scorpions, and that nothing shall by any means hurt them as they go about this endeavor.

It will be my duty in another place to speak of the detail of General Booth's plans, as far as it seems useful for us to consider them. Our business this morning is with the emphatic reliance which the Saviour places upon men's enthusiasm for mankind, in his promises of that coming kingdom to which we look forward. In the contrast between the races of men, it is generally supposed that the people of that race who were called the descendants of Shem, of that race by whom he was himself surrounded, have more of that working enthusiasm than has fallen to the share of the great Aryan race of which we are, or to the Eastern races of which the Chinese and Japanese are, the best representatives, or to that race which has always been at the bottom, which makes up the nations of Africa. Thus it is observed that all the religions of the world have come from Western or Southern Asia, and a great deal more than is worth while has been made of this coincidence. For myself, I suppose that religion is the natural tie between the child and the father. I suppose that it expresses the natural relation of man with God. And I do not believe, therefore, that there was any more religion in Abraham than there was in Massasoit, or in Cetewayo, or in Abraham Lincoln. The mere accidental expression must not be overstated. But with such speculation we have here little to do. Let us rather notice that there has been enthusiasm enough in our race to do everything that the Scripture gives in the list of the triumphs of the children of Abraham. The men of our race, when they were set to do it, "have subdued kingdoms, have wrought righteousness, have obtained promises, have stopped the mouths of lions, have quenched the violence of fire, out of weakness have been made strong, have waxed valiant in the fight, and have put to flight the armies of the aliens." I would not ask for better examples of enthusiasm and daring than were given us by Columbus and his men, or by Cortez and his. I would not ask for enthusiasm more pronounced than that which sent our forefathers to Plymouth, or that which set Ann Lee's disciples to make gardens out of deserts. There is no lack of enthusiasm if there is anybody to start enthusiasm, and you have only to go this afternoon to hear the words spoken in the Salvation Army, or you have only to go to-morrow to see what those people are doing in the slums of Boston, to see that whatever else they lack, they do not lack enthusiasm, because they speak the English language or are born in the Anglo-Saxon race. It is possibly true, however, that a certain timidity or shyness belongs to people of English descent. It is the cause of their inability to express all they feel, so that, when John Foster's son dies, he tells his father that it is only within that half-hour that he has had any conception of how much his father loved him.

We are constantly hearing of such instances. The false shame, as the French call it, of the Englishman, and, to a certain extent, of his successors in New England, keeps his lips closed, so that he does not tell his friend how much he loves him, he does not tell how large are his plans, he is afraid to be called a fanatic, and conceals from the world his very noblest aspirations. All the same, however, it is to be observed that this race goes into crusades under the lead of Peter the Hermit, that it compasses sea and land when it is led by Columbus or by Magellan, or in our times by Hayes or by Greeley. The pent-up enthusiasm which did not find language, exists in some magnificent outburst of concentrated effort. In the instance to which I have alluded, General

Booth is relying upon this concentrated enthusiasm, working under such regulation and discipline as he has established for his army. I do not myself believe that we need here a great deal of that especial form of the Salvation Army. Fortunately for us, we have solved a good many of the problems which England has still to solve, and there has thus resulted a sort of prosperity for each and every class here which in England seems to belong only on the higher circles of their social order. While I recognize, therefore, with gratitude, what these humble and despised people are doing, here in Boston, in New York, and in our other cities, I do not believe we need to call upon them to work any such miracles as General Booth is calling for there. But you and I ought to remember that, for the great problems which are before us now, we have in reserve just such a reservoir, shall I say, of human power, which can do literally what it will in the reformation of the world and the improvement of society, when once it sees what the needs of the social order are, and when once it knows that the good God calls for such miracles.

A venerable friend of ours listened uneasily to some of the poor materialism which tries to account for manhood and its victories by talk about phosphorus and electricity. He waited impatiently till he had a right to speak, and then said, "John, you do not believe that the uprising of America in

1861, when this people as one man swept away all obstacles, — one man, indeed, for union and freedom, — you do not believe that this was nothing but the consentaneous ticking of ten million pendulums! It was the enthusiastic determination of ten million children of God." Now such enthusiasm is a power as distinctly to be relied upon as is the rising of the tide or the flow of a river. And any statesman or reformer does not know the alphabet of his business who does not rely upon it, as the Law to which the God of History has intrusted the advance and enlightenment of his world.

It is desirable to remember this, and to illustrate it, that we may always look forward to large successes. Only those who have scanty resources, finite and fallible, will be satisfied with small plans. "We will abolish slavery," said the Abolitionist. And they did so. "We will make the desert blossom like the rose," said Daniel Boone and Manasseh Cutler. And they did so. "We will cover this land with a net-work of railways," said another forward-looking army of inventors. And they did so. They trod on serpents and scorpions, if you please; but they had that enthusiasm which permits men to do so, — "so that nothing shall by any means hurt you." For the future, we have the same rights to do large things rather than small. "It is often easier to do a great thing than a little one." Thus, when John Adams says that in America every man and woman should have a liberal education, he proposes a condition wholly unknown in his time, wholly unknown in ours, but definite and possible to the power of genuine enthusiasm. When some man tells you that you ought to abolish pauperism, that it is a disease to be trampled out like leprosy or like small-pox, you are not to send him to an insane hospital, but you are to rely on this infinite power, as you address yourselves to the work which so great a purpose demands. Stupendous difficulty? Yes; but, as God orders, I have stupendous power. This power, pent up and available, was given me for use. It is not meant for nothing. We will turn it on this obstacle. The obstacle shall give way. If we are sons and daughters of the Living God, going and coming with his Infinite Commission, we will do something which is worth doing.

We will do something worth doing, — that is the resolution for you and me. We do not call ourselves reformers. We do not, I suppose, regard ourselves as professed philanthropists. There are things which we should be glad to have done, which we leave for other people to do. Thus, we should be very glad to have Jerusalem taken out of the hands of the Turk. But we do not go about preaching to people to ask them to go to Jerusalem and drive the Turk out. When we ask people to take the cross and bear it, we have other objects nearer home. It is much more my business and yours to see that Boston is decently governed than that Jerusalem is. And very likely the place that you and I have in that business may be in teaching a child to sew in the Parmenter Street Chapel, or taking a newsboy on a sleigh-ride around the Reservoir. But sewing or sleigh-ride, ward-meeting or public speech, you and I are not going to see any of the large successes, unless we ally ourselves with large plans, and unless we rely on this reserved enthusiasm which works the miracles. We shall not make people temperate by taking slates to them, and calculating that whiskey costs more than clothing. We shall make them temperate by quickening the divine fire till it blazes, by giving it new fuel that it may burn higher, by piling into it this thing or that which tempts to wrong, so that the temptations may be destroyed. This sacrifice, by the way, is what "enthusiasm" originally meant. It is what the sceptics and machine people cannot understand. But it is involved in the great principle which wins all the victories.

Thank God, and thank the enthusiasm of our fanatic fathers, we have not the problem which General Booth is facing so gallantly. Not one man, woman, or child in Boston slept last night in quarters as noisome and wretched as fifty thousand people in London were trying to sleep in at the same time. But there were bad enough places here. I can show you — any leader in the ministry at large or in the Salvation Army can show you — places where people did sleep which it shall make you weep to see. And we have our other failures, for which no fathers have provided. Diseases running rampant, which might be trampled out. Ignorance, almost proud that it is ignorant. Labor, crowded just where it is not wanted, and wanted just where it does not come. Wealth untold, in the hands of those who are so stupid that they do not know that wealth, as wealth, is merely vulgar. Learning untold, in the brains of people who do not know that learning is only a morbid disease, unless it is shared to the last fraction with all sorts and conditions of men. Life in the midst of plenty, which does not know how to live. A country drunk with its own prosperity, which hardly knows how to use its riches, and yet, like other drunkards, staggers on and asks for more. Now, it is over such mountains, and in spite of them, that you and I, and others like us, are to carry the car of the Living God. He means that his treasures shall be scattered right and left. He means that health shall be as sure in every home as it is now in the palaces of favored princes. He means that ripe learning, and the joy of understanding his work, shall be everywhere, as certain as it is now in colleges or in libraries. He means that no man shall sulk in a miser's wretchedness, counting his gold and weighing his silver, but that that miser, most wretched of all, shall be exalted to the luxury of leading, teaching, spending, relieving, and receiving the blessings of his fellow-men. You and I, among others, are set to this business of hewing down such mountains and building up such valleys.

We shall succeed if we aim high enough. We shall fail if we accept things as they are. We shall succeed if we trust the wave of enthusiasm of those who are born from God, and try to live and move and have their being in him. We shall fail if we only find fault with other people's plans, — if we do nothing but say the work is hard to do. Certainly we shall fail if we suppose that wrong will right itself; that falsehood will teach people to tell the truth; that bribery will make man pure; or, in general, if we think it wise to let things alone. And, for ourselves, we shall be strong and confident if we seek God to help us; — for then we shall find him. We shall be faint and weak if we do not seek him, for then even his Omnipotence will find it hard to set our pulses beating. What you and I need is with each breath of life to come "Nearer, Great God, to thee," — not simply, as the hymn says so well, in any flight through space, but in these relations of life, just as intimate, of Monday morning and Tuesday afternoon. I am talking to a stranger in the street-car. Yes — and the God of Heaven is the third person in the interview. I am standing at an open grave. Yes — and the Father of perfect love holds me, so that I may not die in my wretchedness. I am before an audience which distrusts and doubts me. Speak by my lips, Father, and compel them to understand. Or I have this child to amuse, who is fretful and overbearing. Father of my life, show me how to attend to her as wisely as you have cared for me. The man who has fairly sought for this Infinite Companionship has found it. That man has found that the lions in the way receded before him. He has not found that the gnats from the foliage, or the little ants from their burrows, or the beetles who flew across his path, really hindered him. He trod on serpents and scorpions, and they did not hurt him. He did not succeed by this method, or that method. It was not that one plan was so much wiser than another, for this was no affair of plan. It was not one or another contrivance of machinery. It was a question how Infinite Power should be brought to compel the machinery. And this man, in his unselfish enthusiasm, was the living partner of the Living God!

WHAT THINK YE OF CHRIST?

"What think ye of the Christ? whose son is he?"
MATTHEW xxii. 42.

THE first half of this text was selected by Father Ignatius for his discourse, when he preached in this pulpit three weeks since. With that curious indifference to historical accuracy which seems to stamp enthusiasts, he omitted the last half of the text, and made no illusion to the incident described. This was a pity. For, as he wanted to interest us in the real history of Jesus, it would have seemed natural to tell us why Jesus asked the question of the text on this occasion, when he never asked it of the same people on any other occasion. For the subject Father Ignatius was discussing, it is a very curious observation that the Saviour himself was so indifferent as to men's questions or thoughts about him. He once asked his apostles what the multitude thought about him. On this occasion he does not even speak of himself. He asks a general question as to the Messiah whom all expected. Whose son shall the Messiah be? Must he be David's son? "Whose son is he, — the son of David or the son of God?" For the rest he said squarely, "It is my Father who does the works. It is the Holy Spirit who speaks the word. If any man blasphemes me, he may be forgiven." He even chides his disciples because they can do nothing without him. He sinks his own personality. As Paul says so well, "He makes himself of no reputation. He takes upon himself the form of a servant." You might say he is quite indifferent how men define his nature or his position if only they will follow him.

You might say he is absolutely indifferent to this question, "What think ye of Christ?" which we are now told is the most important question of all. If you read the four Gospels for the first time, and merely addressed yourself to the question of what he did think important, you would say at once that his whole heart and soul were put on bringing in the kingdom of God.

There is, as I said, one and only one central passage where he gave to us his own statement. Curiously enough, again, this passage is now coolly rejected by those who are most eager to extol his authority. When they were all driven out of Galilee, when they had taken refuge in a foreign dominion, he asked the twelve who they thought he was. Simon Peter promptly answered, "Thou art the Christ, the son of the living God." Jesus praised him for the answer; he said he would build his Church on that answer, — that that answer should be sufficient for the foundation of the Church, and that on a church so built hell would have no power. "Thou art the Christ, the son of the living God."

How extraordinary it is, if Peter made the wrong reply, — as we are now told he did, — if Peter should have said, "Thou art the living God," as the creeds of the fifth century would have him say! How extraordinary that this central occasion should have been lost, nay, should have been worse than lost! How extraordinary that Peter should say Jesus was the son of God, if he were God himself! This failure can only be accounted for on the ground which our friend Dr. Huntington takes, the Bishop of Syracuse, when he says that Peter did not himself then know who the Saviour was, and only found out after the Saviour had died.

As to our text itself, it is only interesting in what I may almost call the dramatic sequence of events; because it illustrates the Saviour's steady determination to put down, even by ridicule, that Jewish prejudice which made out the children of Abraham to be the only people in the world worth thinking of. I have read the whole passage, as Father Ignatius did not, that you might see this determination of his, and how important it is that the two parts of this text shall be kept together. Here was this Jewish superstition, that when God chose to send his messenger, when the Christ should come, he must be of the line of David. The same superstition shows itself in those long genealogies with which the Gospels of Matthew and of Luke begin, in which, by different lines, Christ's birth is traced back to David, to show that he fulfilled the Jewish condition. But the Saviour himself shows indifference to this tradition. When they say at once that the Christ must be the son of David, he says in reply, "Why, David calls him 'Lord.' David admits that he himself is inferior to any one who comes direct from God. And do you mean that David requires a genealogical descent from himself of one who is to be the King of kings, and Lord of lords?" The incident is only one of many on which he presses hard upon that provincialism of the Jews. "God is able of these stones to raise up children unto Abraham." "The publicans and the harlots shall go into the kingdom of heaven before you." Yes, the Gentiles, who are like beggars out in the highway, they shall be received at the feast when the children of Abraham are left out. Such are the parables and such the epigrams by which this local provincialism is rebuked. And what is offered on the other side? The grandeur of a true-born son of God. The light and life and glory and victory which will certainly come when a child of God partakes of the divine nature, as we all may, enters into the life of God, is inspired by the Holy Spirit, and works the miracles, therefore, which the Holy Spirit may command. There is one and another curious phrase, to show how broadly Jesus interprets this title of "son," and how much he means by the central word "father." In another interview in this same temple, he quotes from the 82d Psalm the words in which those are called gods to whom the word of God came, — " Is it not written in your law, I said, ye are gods?" And then he puts squarely the question, which neither Father Ignatius nor any of his school ever condescends to answer, " If he called them gods unto whom the word of God came (and the Scripture cannot be broken), say ye of him whom the Father sanctified and sent into the world, Thou blasphemest, because I said I am the son of God?" If God is our father, we are all God's sons or God's daughters. And then, as the centre of expostulation and entreaty, he begs us to recognize the greatness of this calling, to be true to the spirit which inspires us, and as princes of the blood royal to live in the Father's house, and to go about the Father's business. Not unwilling to take the fond phrases, in which, with more or less distinctness, old prophets have spoken of the Messiah, he is willing to accept such terms as "First-born," "First-begotten," "Best beloved;" but always there is the determination that we shall understand that where there is a first-born son, there are other children, and that he opens for us the inheritance which he begs us all to claim.

What think ye of the Christ, then? The gospel answer to this question is, that the Christ is the Son of God.

Thou art the Christ, the Son of the living God, is indeed the motto for the corner-stone of the church, as he said it was.

And any effort to make it out that more was concealed behind this phrase than it expresses, is an effort which re-acts against him who makes it. The Church herself stopped dead in her amazing advance of the early centuries. She failed in her real duty, and sunk back into an "establishment" just so soon as she began to worship him. Then it was that she turned away from the work which he assigned to her, which was to bring in the Kingdom of God.

"I am your master," he said. Yes. "You are to follow me, and I am your leader." Yes. "But you are to seek the Spirit of God to enliven you and give you strength. And, in fact, I go away that that Spirit may more surely possess you." Nay, his word is so strong as this, "If I do not go away, the Comforter will not come to you."

So careful is he to efface himself from the worship of the church. He brings the wandering child to the Father's feet, and then goes away, that he may leave him there.

I. There are thirty different texts in which the Saviour more or less distinctly defines Christian discipleship. Such is the statement to Nicodemus, the earliest of them: "Except a man be born again he cannot see the Kingdom of God." I need not read them. It will be a better exercise for you to copy them from your own Bibles yourselves. In those thirty texts he speaks three times of their believing on him. In all of them he speaks as to those who love him enough to believe him and to follow him. But in not one of them does he lay the least stress on any intellectual process. In not one of them does he open the question as to what they think of him, or what honor they shall pay to him. He offered himself as our Master, and left us his unfinished work. He says to us, "If you obey me, you will follow me." He proved his affection in his death. And he says, "If you believe in me, you will love me." He means that we shall unite in such love, and he says: "If you love me, you will love each other." In all these statements he speaks as one who would bring in the Kingdom of the Living God. Of himself he says almost nothing. But when he does speak, it is to say that he represents that Living God as his anointed and well-beloved Son.

II. When you come, in the Testament, to the apostles' definition of Christianity you find the same statement. They are building on the foundation. The foundation is: "Thou art the Christ, the Son of the living God." They are never tempted, right hand or left hand, to make any other statement. They baptize into the name of Jesus the Christ, Jesus the Saviour. They make no pretence that this Jesus is very God of very God. Their one central thought is the building up a church of God's children; of the sons of God and of his daughters.

To these sons and daughters they say, "Here is God, God is near: enter his Kingdom." To bind them together, they baptize them in the name of Jesus Christ, the first begotten of their company, the best beloved Son of God, who has called them from darkness into light. And they call upon each and all to receive, as he received, the present Spirit of God, to live in that Spirit, to walk in that Spirit, to go and to come as themselves, God's children. "Walk worthy of the *calling* with which ye are called," as that Son of God walked, who died that you might come into your Father's home, and he into yours.

III. What the church thought of Christ, in the first centuries after the apostles, has appeared very distinctly in late years, in the discovery of the early Catechism, to which the name of the twelve apostles was given. It was the Catechism taught to new converts before they received the supper. Its language at the supper, for instance, shows that that was then a simple service of thanksgiving: —

"Concerning the Eucharist, thus give thanks; first concerning the cup: We thank thee, our Father, for the holy wine of David thy servant, which thou hast made known to us through Jesus thy servant; to thee be the glory forever. And concerning the broken bread: We thank thee, our Father, for the life and knowledge which thou hast made known to us through Jesus thy servant; to thee be the glory forever." All worship, all prayers, are addressed to the Father. Jesus is his servant, whom he has sent as a teacher. He is as he was in Peter's word, "The son of the living God." It is on this rock that the church of that day knew that it was standing.

And so long as they sought what he sought, — to bring in the Kingdom of God, — the church triumphed, with a sway which no philosophy understood, and which no martyrdom set backward. But then, alas! that came which he foresaw. Ah! it is so much easier to worship him than to follow him. "Many will say 'Lord, Lord,' who do not the things that I say." While the church was willing to do the things he said, though it was the communion of the poor and the ignorant, of the weak and foolish, it triumphed. In those days it had no name for him other than his own, none but the anointed of God, brother of our brotherhood, first heir of inheritance, Son of God, well beloved, first-born, Master, and Lord. But it was not so easy to do as one would be done by; it was not so easy to feed the poor and to welcome the leper; it was not so easy to live in the brotherhood of humanity. It was a great deal easier to fall down and worship him, as he had never asked them to do; vastly easier to call him very God of very God, as he never said he was; easier to say he made the worlds, as he did not. Weary of that harder service, weary of the way of thorns, the church made its compact with the world. And from that day to this day, its formal creeds have thrown upon him the burden of the sins of mankind, and have given to him the homage which he gave to his Father.

IV. Yet he was never left without a witness. Central in all testimonies were the four Gospels, which would not change. Steadily they say that he is the Anointed — the Son of the living God. There was the confessed refusal of all Palestine, where he lived and died, to give him any other name, whether men were his followers or no. There were such simple Christians as those in the valleys of the Alps, who would never say that the Son was the Father, and did not know what was meant when men said it.

More and more, as Galileo's tube opened the sky, as this world took its proper little place in the universe, as it showed itself, a little speck of dust floating in space, by the same law which ruled planets, suns, and constellations; more and more did men ask themselves what the creed of the church meant when it said that Jesus of Nazareth made all the worlds; or what it meant when it said that the very God of the universe even, left the universe to stand on the deck of a fishing-boat at Capernaum. More and more the devout thought of the world went back to the simple statement of the four Gospels, and recognized and found its Saviour, as never before, when it accepted him again as the well-beloved Son of the Living God, commissioned and anointed to bring in the Kingdom of God.

This is the statement of his work and his position which will stand, because it is his own statement. For us, our place is gratitude and loyalty. "What is that to thee?" he said to Peter once, when Peter stepped too far in a question, — "what is that to thee? Follow thou me."

And that is what he would say to us if we could put to him some of our speculative questions, — these conundrums which the theologians hand about so glibly, — "What is that to thee? Follow thou me." Whoever will take the Saviour of men, in his work of saving them from their sins, whoever will try the great experiment of prayer, and the other experiment of sacrifice, as this Leader of men bids him try one and the other, comes to the certainty that here is a Leader who knows how to lead, who knows what he is talking about, and who shows the way. Whoever follows, though with trembling foot and fickle faith, follows each day more hopefully and strongly, and knows that this is no finite guess that he is working on; he knows that he has God's law for the affairs of men; this time he is sure of his Leader. This Leader is from God, commissioned by him, inspired by him, and sustained by him. He who follows that Leader, comes to believe that Leader, and to live in his Life. As the Saviour prays, he prays. As the Saviour trusts, he trusts. As the Saviour listens, he listens. He comes to know that the living God, the living Power of the Universe, loves and strengthens every child of earth. They are his children, partakers of his nature, and alive with his life. Such a child of God, who has followed to such purpose the Son of God well-beloved, dares the great experiment of the Holy Spirit. He lives in God, he moves in God, in God he has his being. He plunges into life, knowing that the living God will sustain him and carry him through. He believes the Master's words, "Lo, I am not alone, for my Father is with me."

"God does not hate me. He loves me." This is the cry of such a disciple. "God does not punish me. He forgives me. God does not forget me as he goes about in his universe. He is here — to-day — this minute. And I — I am not in the darkness. I am in his Light. I am not alone. I am with him. I am not weak. I am in his arms. For I am his child — born of him — as I shall return to him. My life is not of to-day, not of to-morrow, but is forever; it is as the life of God." This is the joy of life — to come to this certainty. And the disciple who is so glad, the disciple who is so certain, cannot find hymn or psalm joyous enough to express his exultation; he cannot frame the word which expresses his gratitude. What can he do but follow loyally, lovingly, heartily, the Leader who has led him, the Teacher who has taught him, the Saviour who has saved him, the Brother who has blessed him. He finds the way of life. He looks, and lo! an Open Door. Thou art indeed the Christ, the Son of the living God.

FIVE QUESTIONS.

"Our Father who art in heaven, hallowed be thy name."
MATT. vi. 9.

I HAVE received a courteous letter from the editor of the "Boston Investigator." This is a newspaper which has existed in Boston, dedicated to what used to be called infidelity, since 1831, and is read, as it says itself, by thousands of men and women who are in the dark about God, and are willing to be enlightened. The letter which I have received is an "open letter to the clergymen of Boston." I will not read it at length now, but I will read the five questions which it puts to all of us.

1. What do you mean by the word "God"?
2. How do you know that there is a God?
3. Where is the dwelling-place of God, or where is heaven?
4. What makes the Bible the word of God?
5. Did God write the Bible, or dictate it, or make it divine after it was written?

Nothing can be more interesting than the fact that such a letter, intelligently drawn and courteously written, is addressed, in good faith, to the preachers of the Christian religion in Boston. It is simply my duty, as it is a pleasure, to reply to it; and there are many reasons why I read the reply here before sending it, as I shall do, to Mr. Washburn.

It would be rather painful to think that one had preached what he thought true in Boston for thirty-five years, and that any person who cared about him was ignorant of his views on these five subjects. But I can well understand that, as there are many different answers possible to each of these five questions, that vague person whom we call "the average reader" might fail to see how those answers connect with each other. That is to say, it may well be that the whole system of religious belief often confuses the inquirer who knows what is one or another detail.

It is interesting to observe that a person who calls himself an infidel puts his questions in about the same way in which they would be put in a theological school by the most conservative of professors. This seems to show that both are making the same inquiry, in much the same spirit and with much the same purpose.

I. The first question, then, is, "What do you mean by 'God'?" My answer is that that word is the word which has, on the whole, been agreed upon by the persons who speak the English language, to denote the infinite Power which appears in all nature. As to the existence of this Power there is no question. Some Power makes what we call storms sweep across the continent, so that snow is falling from the atmosphere while I write these words. Some Power has set the world and sun in such order that on this world it is daylight for a part of the time and darkness for another part of the time. To this Power, the people who use the English language have, on the whole, assigned the name "God;" and I use that word because it is the English word for this Power. Jesus Christ, whom I call the Saviour of men, preferred to use the word "Father" when he spoke of this Power. This was because he definitely and distinctly believed that men and women are of the same nature with this Power. He definitely and distinctly believed, as I believe, that this Power is aware of what men and women do, and assists them in doing it. Just as any man of science would say that gravitation or electricity results from this Power, Jesus Christ said that love, memory, imagination, and any other human attribute come from the Power who rules the universe.

II. The second question is, "How do you know that there is a God?" After my first answer, Mr. Washburn would put this question thus: "How do you know that this Power is conscious of your existence?" For Mr. Washburn and I would agree that there is such a Power in the universe. The general answer which will be made to Mr. Washburn is that all men and women are conscious of the existence of God, unless they have been early prejudiced. It will be said to him that all nations in all times have believed in the existence of a conscious Power above them, and that this general accord of the common sense of men is a strong reason for belief that such a Power exists. At all events, it will be said, a feeling naturally impressed in all human hearts must be taken as fundamental in any human discussions. It seems to me that this statement is worth a great deal, and I should find it very hard to parry it if it were made against me in argument. But I know perfectly well that Mr. Washburn will say in reply what he has a right to say, — that he has no such sentiment. He will say that he never had any such sentiment, and that therefore when I appeal to the consciousness of the human race, I make an appeal which he is not bound to respect. I think, as a matter of logic, he has a right to make this reply.

For myself, however, it is a matter of the greatest interest to observe that here live, upon this world, millions and millions and millions of men, beasts, birds, fishes, and insects who are conscious of their own existence and aware of the existence of others. Even a fly knows that he is alive, and knows that other flies are alive around him. Observing this, there is to me something preposterous beyond language in the assumption that every other world goes about its own business without such life — such conscious life; that this element which we call life, this element of consciousness, is unknown outside this world — in all that universe. To suppose that on this little speck there are some millions of beings, loving, hating, fearing, resolving, worshipping, acting, and creating from conscious impulse, and then to suppose that everywhere outside of this speck there is no loving, no hating, no fearing, no hoping, no worshipping, and no creating, is to me so sublimely absurd that I find it difficult to conceive that other people hold that impression. To go a little farther, I find that I, with five senses, and five senses only, by which to communicate with outside nature, am able to form a definite and well-conceived opinion regarding many things which are passing in stars whose distance from me is almost beyond statement. I find myself able to go back into the past through ages indefinite, even though you say I may not go forward into the future; I find that a little five-sensed man like me is capable of this almost infinite range in his life. As this is so, I find it absolutely impossible to think that the Power who moves worlds, makes suns shine or not shine, and creates me and creates everything around me, is doing this without thought, without hope, without life — that that Power is not He, but is It — that that Power is an unconscious power.

If this Power knows what he is about, if he is conscious of his work, he knows more or less about me, about what I am about, and about what my work is.

I do not suppose that the average savage of early days would have made this statement in exactly this form; but I do suppose that, from the beginning, a certain sympathy between the processes of nature, as we call them, and the processes of a man's life has led the average savage or the average sage to the feeling that there is possible conversation or communion between the Infinite Being and the finite being. That is, prayer or communion between the two comes from the certainty that nature, or God, is interested in man. If God knows about me and cares for me, — if I am of his nature, — I know something about him and certainly I care for him.

Such mutual consciousness may of course be expressed in a thousand ways. But there are, however, simple experiments which the world has been trying for tens of thousands of years, — probably for hundreds of thousands of years, — which have brought men to the conviction of to-day. If God is conscious of my existence, if I have, to say the least, a suspicion that he exists, I can try the experiment. Even if I were as badly off as a fishing-vessel in a fog, and knew not where I was, I could blow the steam-whistle or sound the horn hour after hour of the tedious night. And if, of a sudden, I heard whistle or horn in reply, I should know that I was not alone, but that there was some other intelligence at hand. It is thus in the power of any child of God to try the great experiment. He can come to God in prayer. Day in and out, month in and out, year in and out, he can tell him everything — one's hopes and fears, one's joys and sorrows. The men who have tried this great experiment in hundreds of thousands of years are, on the whole, agreed that these prayers have been answered. They are, on the whole, sure that from the infinite Power which rules all life new power has come to them in proportion as they have entered into his life, his purpose, and his affair. If they have lived as sons of God, partakers of his nature, they have more and more believed that he is their Father, and they have had more and more of the infinite strength which controls the world. On the whole, taking a long sweep of the circle for the calculation, those children of God who have tried to walk with God, to carry out such laws as they have found him give, and to give themselves to such purposes as they believe to be his purposes, have been the men and women who have succeeded in this world. And they are the very men and women who have begged other persons to enter into the same communion with him.

Of such prayer the simplest form and the best for a doubtful beginner, if you please, is that old form, often repeated, "O God, if there be a God, help my soul, if I have a soul!" This is quoted sometimes as if it were matter for ridicule. It seems to me a yearning appeal of a heart which has been chilled, of a soul whose senses have been stunned, of a child of God who, by some fatal or hellish ingenuity, has been shut up in a prison where he could not see the heavens nor enjoy the life of the earth. Beginning with a prayer as simple, — "Lord, I believe; help thou mine unbelief," — an unprejudiced child of God, with every sense open for an answer, eager to live life larger and larger, comes out — perhaps to-day, perhaps to-morrow, perhaps next year, perhaps after some shock or crisis of being — into infinite life, is no longer hemmed in in the petty work of five human senses, but partakes of the divine nature and goes about his God's infinite concerns.

If, as he lives, he is born as a little child every day, the prayer becomes absolute intimacy. He nestles in this Father's arms as a glad child in her mother's. "Father dear, now they have all gone, now we are alone, tell me something. What is there to-day? What are you doing, Father dear? What can I do — can I not help somewhere? Oh, do let me tell you, dear Father, what a time I have had. I was all broken to pieces, I was so angry. And then just in time I remembered. I remembered how good you are, and I would not give way. But please show me how I am to pull through." Men come into the real presence, and they are sure that the central Love of the universe sustains them. Here, then, is my answer to the second question.

III. And in these statements is the answer to the next question of our series: "Where is heaven?" Heaven is the universe of space. Heaven is here, as it is in the planet Jupiter, or in the worlds which surround the stars of the Pleiades. Wherever is the universal God who rules all nature, wherever is the Power who works for righteousness, there is heaven. When I accept that glad suggestion or impression that I am of that life, that I share that power, that I partake of that divine nature, I am in heaven as God is in heaven. I have not to take the wings of the eagle, I have not to go to the uttermost parts of any unfathomed ocean. God is with me, I am with him. I live and move and have my being in my God; and so I am in heaven. Some poet, not known to me, speaks of

> "That perfect presence of his face
> Which we, for lack of words, call heaven."

It is easy to see that, in the earlier language of barbarous tribes, it was supposed that certain spots in space were more sacred than other spots. But it belongs to the life more abundant, of man who is infinite in his aspirations and infinite in his powers, to discover that there is no such limitation. I shall not put it better than it is put by one of these old Hebrew prophets: "If I ascend to the skies thou art there; if I descend into the depths thou art there; if I take the wings of the morning and dwell in the uttermost parts of the universe, even there shall thy hand lead me, and thy right hand shall hold me."

In a word, every difficulty which has been suggested in these questions, thus far, seems to be a difficulty belonging to the use of crippled language, to the mechanical use of certain words made from things. So soon as man, the child of God, takes into his heart the reality that he is also infinite, and is of the nature of the Power which makes for righteousness, all these separate questions go back to the etymologists and to the dictionaries.

IV., V. The next questions "What is the Bible?" and "Did God write the Bible?" are simpler questions, merely of human history. It happened or it was ordered, under this present law of God, that the Jewish nation, at its best periods, made the worship of an unseen God a central matter, as other nations of their time did not. So when they wrote history or poetry it was history or poetry devout in its statement and expression. It looked toward God. It has so happened, or has been so ordered, that a few of the histories and poems thus written struggled through, as the naturalists say, by the survival of the fittest, where other literature has gone to ruin. It became, therefore, the centre around which formed itself the religious literature of the Western World. This is just as other books of high antiquity have become the centre of the religious expression of the Eastern World.

The early Christians, who had received from Jesus Christ new life and new lessons of life, took and read in their assemblies these religious books of the Hebrew nation to which he belonged. But they wanted much more — to know what he said, and what they said who knew him best. They therefore collected all the written remains which they could find, of those men who had proclaimed his glad tidings. Again, the law of selection preserved some, while others, of course, have disappeared. A council of Christian teachers, held in the beginning of the fourth century, made the selection which we now call the New Testament, in the attempt to say what manuscripts then existing were the words of Christ's companions.

In neither of these books — the Old Testament or the New Testament — is any claim made that they are written by God, or that they are directed by him except as he directs all life. Nor is the claim made in them that his Word cannot be found elsewhere. They do not make any such claim, and if they did it is clear enough that such a claim of itself would not add to the authority. All the more, however, the Bible, as it stands, is the best record of many of the few greatest crises of history. It contains the word of Him who has proved to be the Leader of Life, the Life-giver, and the Saviour. It will therefore hold the place which it has won. For that thing which the world craves as its needs is Life. It craves the closest intimacy it can gain with the God who makes for righteousness. So it clings to the Bible, which tells the steps and records the words of those who have known this absolute intimacy.

It is pathetic enough that such questions can be asked, with such serious dignity, in the year 1892. It is pathetic indeed — it might well make one wretched — to see that even science, even what is called theology, even the organization of churches, should have cramped and hardened as they have the forms of thought and the words in which men speak of infinite truth; pathetic, indeed, that any man or woman who might be exulting in the liberty of the infinite children of an infinite God is thus hampered and distressed by the mechanism of words, so as to be asking what they mean, and hesitating before accepting any answer. Nearly nineteen hundred years since, Jesus Christ said, "God is spirit, and they that worship him must worship him in spirit and in truth." Surely he said, if nobody had said it before, that we are the children of God and are like him; that he is our Father and that we partake his nature. He said, if nobody said it before, "Ye shall be perfect, even as your Father in heaven is perfect." He said, if nobody ever said it before,

"I must go about my Father's business." And if nobody ever said it before, he said that if we are willing to embark in the great purpose of the universe, with the great Power who makes for righteousness, the Power who makes for righteousness strengthens our hearts and quickens our minds and gives to us the victory. And we, summoned by such a call, quickened by such a hope, turn around to ask if this infinite Power of life and love is like Jupiter sitting on Olympus, or like Neptune riding from wave to wave on a chariot. We ask whether certain pages of paper, with certain letters printed upon them with ink, contain his whole law of life and love, and exclude the law whispered in all the winds, written on all the fields, spoken by every voice which the ear can hear, and written over the seas and over the skies.

Do not such appeals as this which I have been reading urge any of us who may have been lukewarm as to the duty of a spiritual and liberal church to send out its glad tidings beyond its own walls? Naturally enough, we hate the propaganda which the Middle Ages set on foot. Naturally enough, the mere word *missions* has tainted itself, as that word *propaganda* is associated with the idea of restriction. But one has only to see how a false definition of the name of God makes men disbelieve in him; how a false claim made for the Bible makes them throw the Bible to the winds; how a mechanical account of the domain of heaven makes them refuse to enter into the infinite heaven of perfect love; one has only to see the evidence of such torpor as follows on the worship of words, and he consecrates himself anew to proclaim the gospel of realities. He swears he will let the world know the glorious truth, as the centuries have revealed it. It can be stated in three words, or it can be expanded through poems and histories. God is with us, and we are with him. As he lives, life is real. We can live in that life. His word speaks to me here and now. And when I hear it and when I find him, I am in his kingdom of a present heaven.

FATHER, SON, AND HOLY SPIRIT.

"Go ye forth and make disciples of all the nations, baptizing them into the name of the Father and of the Son and of the Holy Spirit." MATTHEW xxviii. 19.

THIS baptismal formula is repeated every day of the year in thousands of Christian churches.

But I am afraid that its use is almost absolutely conventional. As one might take the stars and stripes of our flag and say that the flag is the symbol of the country, without asking why the stars are there or why the stripes are there, so I am afraid people repeat these ancient words which refer to Father, Son, and Spirit.

So I am more glad to use them, with that addition which is made to them in one of the ancient doxologies. Here the worshipper sang:

"Glory to the Father, and to the Son, and to the Holy Spirit. As it was in the beginning."

As it was in the beginning.

If you and I could only repeat this formula, as if it were not a formula; if you and I could only use such words, all fresh and alive with the life with which Christ spoke them; if they were

Edward E. Hale.

words which had meaning in them, which had living sap in them, which had red blood in them, — then we could make them the war-cry of the Church or its pæan of victory. But they are neither war-cry nor pæan if they are only repeated decorously, as the requisition of a liturgy.

The trouble is, in all our use of the Gospels, that we fail to see the amazing novelty to those people of the Saviour's statement. So we do not comprehend the sudden start, the flash of light, the determination to live, shall I say, as giants or as angels, in that infinite future which is spread before us. Indeed, it is almost impossible for us to feel this; but we must try, we must use our imaginations. Here is the Saviour in the midst of all sorts of people — Pharisees, Sadducees, Samaritans, Phœnicians, Arabs, Parthians, Greeks, Romans, Egyptians, people who have had all sorts of gods, or who have had no God, one God, or many gods. Some of these gods were what we should call devils. All of them represented force and arbitrary power. They were kings or judges, perhaps they were executioners or magistrates. Everybody was afraid of them. To be afraid of them was a requisite of what was called religion. Religion, indeed, is often defined among the writers of that time as the terror of the inferior in presence of the superior. They went so far, you remember, as to say squarely that "the fear of the

Lord is the beginning of wisdom." Into the midst of the chattering of such worshippers, cold with fear and almost dumb from terror, comes Jesus Christ. And he says, "Whom are you afraid of? What are you afraid of? This Power who maintains this world, and brings you and me into being, — he is our Father. He loves us, and whenever we know him we love him. He cannot help loving us, and we cannot help loving him." When he has to say which commandment of the old law is greatest of them all, it is Moses' instruction, which they had never understood and never fulfilled, that they should love the Lord their God. And the central statement of all he has to say to them is this statement, that God loves them and does not hate them; that God loves them and does not judge them; that God commands them only because he loves them; and that because he loves them God watches over them and cares for them. Nature is really conscious, and is on our side. Now we are used to all this. To us the words "Our Father" and the word "God" have become synonymous, and they mean the same thing when we use them, just as the two words "Lord" and "God" have become synonymous. It was not so then. It was the marvel of marvels. Here is this prophet, — clearly he knows what he is talking about, — and he says nature is not cruel, but she is kind. God is not our King, but our Father. God watches us always, and though we do not know it, his every act and thought are act and thought of love.

Of course, then, in the watchword of the new Church, in its worship, in its baptism, in its proclamation, this word comes foremost. We are not to baptize in the name of Jehovah; not even, observe, in the name of God. We are to show the great reality which we stand for, which lifts our worship above and beyond that of all partial religions. We are to show that it is our Father to whom we come.

Now, who are we who worship? Who are we who proclaim? Who are we who baptize? Who are we who go up and down the world proclaiming these glad tidings? Are we worms of the dust?

No!

Are we so many shell-fish, lying hidden in the sand, over whom there sweep regularly by a fixed order certain ocean tides, which then sweep back again and leave us with no wills of our own, — only to drink in this or that from sunshine or from air?

No!

Are we a set of machines, carefully constructed, with so many bones, so many nerves, so many muscles and sinews, so much blood, so much cartilage, worked by a stationary battery called a brain, which will run fourscore years and then stop running?

No!

In no accurate sense are we the mere creatures of this Father. We are much more. We share his nature. We partake his life. We are his sons and his daughters. His life is our life. His being is our being. His nature is our nature. Let no man say hereafter that this language is too bold, that no man born of woman has shown such love as God shows, such tenderness as God shows, such justice as he shows, which is mercy. No man shall say this who remembers the son of Mary. The revelation which the son of Mary has made to all his brothers and sisters of mankind is, first, that the God of Nature is their Father; and, second, that in the most real and simple use of words, they are his sons as Jesus Christ is — and they are his daughters. So the new Church, when it states its watchword in an epigram, states this reality with the other. Absolute religion is the religion of the Father and his children. It is the religion of the Father and of the Son. It is the religion of the Father and of all his sons and daughters.

It proved convenient afterward for a church of priests to confine its reverence to that first-born Son as he is called. But the Saviour made no such restriction. "Ye shall do greater things than I," he said to his own. He bade all his brethren address "Our Father." First and last, his appeal to them and to us is to those who can claim all his privileges and hold his communion with God; as when at the end he says:

"I ascend to my Father and your Father, to my God and your God."

We are not to come to him in our prayer. We are to pray as he prayed, to his Father and to ours.

"But these things are too wonderful for me." This is the answer which the camel-driver from Parthia makes to Matthew on the Day of Pentecost. This is what the stevedore at Corinth says to Silas on the pier. This is what the philosopher, Seneca, at Rome, says to Paul. "You cannot make us believe," they say, "that this Power who is shaping and moving the world has anything in common with us." Each of them says, " My world is a very small world. His world is infinite." It is, then, the first duty of anybody who proclaims the eternal gospel to meet that difficulty. The Saviour of men does meet it. All his true apostles meet it, and you and I must meet it. It is perfectly true that, judged by our measuring tapes, some things which God does seem very large, and some things which we do seem very small. But to him there is nothing large and nothing small. And we, as we really come to live in him, to move in him, and have our being in him, — as we come to know what it is that we are his children, to believe in the Father and in the Son, — we shall come to know that to child and Father there is one life in each and in both. It is one Spirit which inspires the action which we call "large," and it is the same Spirit which inspires the action which we call "small." Here is this poor mother holding her sick baby in her arms. Hour after hour, day after day, she cares for the child with unvarying and unquestioning love. The child does not thank her, cannot thank her, does not want to thank her. But the mother loves still, loves without question, loves without reward. What dictates such sacrifice? It is the same Spirit of Love which sets the universe in motion. It is the Spirit of Love which clothes the world in exquisite beauty, so that the poets may well sing that the angels delight to look on it from afar. It is the same Spirit of Love which flavors the fruit and colors the flower. That Spirit inspires that mother through the dark watches of the night and through the long hours of the day, so that that love is a perfect love and her sacrifice is unfaltering. You shall not say it is any lesser spirit. This display of this Holy Spirit, this visible victory on that little scene, as you call it, between the whitewashed walls of an attic, is as grand, as noble, as infinite, as is that other display when worlds are called into visible being. The one is perfect, and the other is perfect. The newborn Church means to assert this; it means to assert, not simply the greatness of man's origin, but the dignity of his life. He is engaged here on affairs to which the Lord of lords and King of kings has commissioned him. For those affairs that King of kings and God of gods has commissioned him and inspired him. It is his Spirit, the Infinite and Holy Spirit which rules that universe. It is the same Spirit which quickens the kiss which this mother gives her child. Her affair, also, is infinite, and her love is infinite love.

In the beginning these early teachers meant to express this in their watchword, and that watchword meant this then, when they proclaimed the Father, the Son, and the Holy Spirit.

And that is what we mean now when we give glory to the Father, and the Son, and the Holy Spirit, " as it was in the beginning."

A very curious study is that historical examination which shows how this simple rallying-cry was transformed into the mechanical and dead church doctrine called the Trinity, as held in the Dark Ages. Egypt had its triads of gods, such as Osiris, Isis, and Horus, which in a fashion were one God. And when the modest Christian school appeared in Alexandria, it was not hard to confuse their simple three, Father, Child, and Spirit, into the sonorous phrases which describe three adorable persons as all three one God. Easier still, when Constantine folded Christianity in his arms and almost stifled her in the embrace, for him to grant any honors, any statement of deity, to the Jesus Christ who was crucified three centuries before, if, by that easy bargain, he might strike out from the new-born religion those fatal statements that all men were brethren, and that every man was son of God.

It is no business of ours, however, to go again into that fatal story of the Dark Ages. Thanks to the Christian Reformation and to reformation upon reformation which has sprung from it, the Dark Ages are over, and we live in the light again, or at least in the early dawn. The church doctrine of the Trinity died the day Galileo pointed his telescope at Jupiter. For us to-day, then, one of the necessities is to give glory to the divinity of man, as they did in the beginning. When we speak of the divinity of human nature, we do not confine it to the divinity of Jesus Christ, who came and went in Palestine for thirty-three years. We are talking of the infinite power of all the sons of God, and of all his daughters. We are talking of the infinite and eternal life. We are talking of the range of their duties, of the range of their possibilities, of the range of their successes, of the range of their joys. This is it to give glory to the child of God as it was in the beginning.

And in saying this I am only speaking of one detail of what would be for the higher and better life of mankind, if the Church of Christ to-day would *do* what it *says* in the decorous lip-service of a thousand different forms. It is very true that each age likes to prepare its own symbols, each likes to make its own statements. Nay, each man does this thing. Our dear friend Freeman Clarke used to say that he had reduced the whole to the four words, "Love God, love man." These make an admirable watchword, but of course they require the statement of what you mean by God, and the other statement of what you mean by man. They suppose, that is, that nineteen centuries have brought up the world to the knowledge that God is our Father, and to the knowledge that man is the son of God, is the well-beloved son of God; that man partakes his nature, enters into his work, and enjoys his joy. For myself, I enjoy Paul's phrase, when he says that the abiding elements of life are faith and hope and love.

The French Socialists have taken the phrase "Liberty, equality, fraternity." The English Chartists, the Odd Fellows, the Sons of Temperance, — every leading organization, — has in like wise taken modern words to state its requisition of the times, and to try to turn a fresh corner of the diamond, which has not been rubbed, to do the cutting of the living hour. In every such effort to freshen men's thought and quicken their intelligence, something, certainly, is gained. But all of them involve certain eternal principles. And I say again, if the Church, when it mumbles over these principles in ancient language, could be electrified by some flash from heaven, or quickened by some explosion of earthly dynamite, or roused by some voice of living prophet, to do the thing which she says that she believes, in that day the Kingdom of Heaven would come. Imagine, if you can, a world in which men should go and come with this sense, that nature is on their side and is not against them; a world in which a man shall rejoice in the snow-storm, in the tempest, in the rush of the tide upon the beach, as a child rejoices in the opening of a snowdrop or the perfume of a rose. Imagine a world in which a man who goes forth to his daily duty shall know that God is with him, is present life, strength, comfort, and joy. It is a world in which he does not suppose that a cruel God is pursuing him to punish him. It is a world in which he does not suppose that a critical or cynical God is weighing him on the scales, to snap him off the balance when he is done with him, because he is mean or imperfect. It is a world in which he knows that if he will only use that which is given him, if he will only resolutely eat the manna which falls to-day, it shall be to him for tonic if not for food, it shall give him strength if it do not give him joy. It is a world in which he studies the forces of God, which he has not understood till now, and lo! he finds that lightning is not the engine of God's wrath, but that it is the humble servant of his own convenience and pleasure! He finds that the tempest is not the punishment of man's sins, but that it is to work the wonders of God's present love. The new life, the heart and courage for daily duty, which shall make men do their work — why, as God does his work, gladly, heartily, and of course successfully, is the life which belongs to the world of our Father. It will come the moment when the world really believes in " Our Father." I suppose that that sense of God's love must come first. But it is not impossible for those to see what will come next, who have read the four Gospels. Those who have some touch or sense of the Saviour's life can imagine at least what is to come to the world when men understand as well what it is to believe in the sonship of all God's children. To go about your daily business, as we say here so often, as a prince of the blood royal. This is to share the joy of God; it is to use the strength of God. To forget that any cynic or any fool or any creed ever said that we were born in sin and conceived in iniquity; to forget that any priest or any knave ever proclaimed the folly that we were worms of the dust, and were to cry, "Vile, vile!" or, better than this, to grow up, as I have known children in this church to grow up, utterly ignorant that there ever was such folly or cynicism, which put into words such infinite depreciations of the sons of God, and of his daughters. All this is to give energy of life and hope to the work of this world; yes, and, let me say, to its pleasures; to make of the work a divine offering, new every morning and fresh every evening; and make the pleasures, as well, to be so many steps in the advance of these princes and princesses, as they go forward, indeed, from life to life, from joy to joy, and from glory to glory. This vision seems somewhat dim, and men take it as less possible than that other vision. God reveals himself as our Father with every morning. And the glory and dignity of the sons of God scattered this world over has no such visible or tangible representation. But the Saviour was such a visible representation. Apostles, prophets, and martyrs have all lived and died in the certainty that this vision is to become more real and more to every generation. Every noble life makes the vision more certain. Every unselfish death makes us apprehend better what is its range and infinitude. So that we may well believe that, as the Church casts off its hypocrisies, treads under foot its shams, and makes its liturgies real, the Church herself shall succeed in proclaiming to all children of sorrow, as she has called them, the infinite reality that they are really sons and daughters of the living God.

Then, and perhaps not till then, will Church and world know what men have been saying when, in a half-stupid, half-mechanical way, they have pretended that they have believed in the Holy Spirit.

One spirit with God who loves the world and the same spirit in the hearts of men and women whom he loves and who loves him; to go and come in my daily affair as God goes and comes in his; in the same Holy Spirit, as joyous, as pure, as unselfish, as infinite, — this is what I say is possible when I baptize a little child in the name of the Father and of the Son and of the Holy Spirit. This is what I say is possible when, with my head bent, I repeat the Apostles' Creed, and say that I believe in the Holy Spirit. There is a much greater reality than saying I believe it, and that reality comes to me when I live in that Spirit, when it inspires me, when it gives me the strength of an infinite child of an infinite God, when it gives to my daily duty the breadth and range of some infinite affair. Then it shows me that the consequences of that duty shall sweep through all time and to them there shall be no distance. It shows to me that the success of to-day's endeavor is not simply the cheer in my own household or the comfort of my own friend, though that is no trifle. It is success ranging through all the world and touching all time; for here is the success, here is the victory, of the Holy Spirit of God himself. This is the spirit in which he moves the worlds and sets them in order. It is in this spirit that his sons and daughters live. They are one in him, he is one with them. This is it to live and move and have my being in my God.

HOW IMMORTALS LIVE.

"Things which eye saw not, and ear heard not, and which entered not into the heart of man, whatsoever things God prepared for them that love him. Unto us God revealed them through the Spirit: for the Spirit searcheth all things, yea, the deep things of God."

1 Cor. ii. 9, 10.

"IT is one thing to say one believes in immortality. It is quite another to live as an immortal."

I heard Mr. John Weiss say this in a sermon nearly fifty years ago. I can use no better words now to state the difference between two habits of life and expression. The truth involved is shown in the lives of all the men of infinite experience.

Think how little there is in the four Gospels which can be cited in words, to a person uneasy about infinite life, as one cites an argument. There is no demonstration of immortality suggested or even attempted. There is that difficult and hardly intelligible rejoinder to the Sadducees, where it would seem as if some ready epigram had been mistaken and lifted into the place of an argument. And this is the only approach to what we call demonstration. On the other hand, every important conversation takes immortality absolutely for granted. It is a reality where no argument is needed. It has been settled once and forever. You do not argue about it, you do not prove it, any more than you prove the existence of air or the pressure of gravitation. What one does see — and it is the central pulse of the intense vitality of the Gospels — is this, that Jesus lives as an immortal lives. He is always looking out into infinite life. Food, raiment, shelter, always take a secondary and inferior place. Love, society, — faith, prayer, — hope, heaven, these are the primary matters. These are what one talks about, thinks about, and lives for. He does not so much as say that he believes in immortality, or that they must. But he lives as you know an immortal would live, and he takes it for granted that you will.

I do not regard this as merely an illustration of his evident dislike of talk where it is contrasted with work. That is clear all along, that he detests the people of eager expression, who say, Lord, Lord, but do not the things which he says. There is much more than this. You will find, I think, that just in proportion to the largeness of any one's life, that person refrains from talking about life in heaven, as if he could describe it, or make it evident to the senses.

To compare it with a very small thing, it is only the poor critics, people who are very ignorant of music or of other fine art, who undertake to explain to you in words the power which a noble symphony has over one, or a perfect statue. Lord

Byron ridicules them as those who "describe the indescribable."

It is on a scale vastly larger than this that those people show their own absurdity who undertake to make heaven visible to us, or its language audible. The precise truth for which we want expression is this: that whereas here life is fettered and imprisoned within the somewhat hard control of five senses, the infinite life is not so fettered or controlled. Infinite means unbounded. When Dean Mansell wrote his book on "The Limitations of Religious Enquiry," Dr. Hedge said to me, "Why does the man want to talk about the limitations of that which is unlimited?" And one feels the same surprise, not to say disgust, when one reads in the Koran of Mahomet about the roses and the rubies, the pearls and the feasts, the houries and the djins, which and who make up the heaven to which the true Musselman is invited. Or take the Book of Revelation, with which the Bible ends. The poetry of that book is simply magnificent, when it tells you of thousands and thousands which no man can number; when it tells you of voices which no one can pretend to interpret or understand. But when the language turns to numbering and interpreting, it fails. We come to visions of four square cities measured by measuring-rods, and built upon stones whose mineralogy is explained to us, and we turn the page uneasily and seek for more of the other kind. All this is to say that audible language is, from its very nature, earthly and finite. So far as it goes, it goes very well, but woe to him who tries to make it go farther. My horse or my ass may bear me well to the shore of the infinite ocean, but woe to me if I try to make him carry me over. Human language is necessarily confined to the affairs of the five senses. When it tries to describe the realities which are noted by a thousand senses outside their range, human language of necessity breaks down.

But human life is not limited within five senses. I lie in my bed at midnight: I hear nothing, I see nothing, I taste nothing, I smell nothing, indeed, I feel nothing but the even temperature of 98° Fahr., maintained in my body between the blankets and the mattress; so little do my five senses help me there. But my life, all the same, is taking an unbounded range, if I choose, in memory or in hope, in prayer or in faith, or in the absolutely unlimited sweep of love. I am living, if I choose, in a range of being which does not want to express itself in English words, or German words, or Latin words. It is perfectly indifferent to such earthy, wooden, carnal, clumsy, finite expressions. I would as soon get out of bed and light the lamp and find canvas and an easel and try to paint a picture there, of my love or my aspiration, with colors called Antwerp blue or rose madder and flake white, as undertake to express the same aspiration or the same love in two hundred and fifty words, of which the philologists tell me that fifty-seven per cent. are derived from the Saxon, twenty-two from the Latin, and the rest from the Keltic or the Icelandic or from somewhere else. All that is of the earth, earthy. The word is as earthy as the pigment. And here is the essential reason why any master of life will not fool with these clumsy expressions.

"Whereunto shall I liken the kingdom of God?" This is the groan of the Saviour, indignant because people want to have infinite realities clamped and cramped in human language. It is the reason why all poets tell you that there are more realities in heaven and earth than your written philosophy pretends to. I may say in passing, as of an illustration not very important, that in this truth we find the reason for the utter futility and ghastly dulness of the people who call themselves the spiritualists of to-day.

To live as an immortal lives is a very different matter. How often in history a great man or woman, true child of God, has done God's work as God himself might do it, who had no power of describing the deed when it was done. Years after him, — centuries after, — this poet or that, this artist or that, strives, unequal, to describe or to represent the deed itself, which has long before been approved by all the sons of God as being indeed divine. Arnold of Winkelried rushes forward on the Austrian lances with the cry, "Make way for Liberty!"

In another language, five hundred years after, an English poet tells the story. But the divine deed, of course, is the Swiss peasant's who gave his life a ransom for many.

Perhaps the best things in poetry are its successes, when it does show how what we call the most insignificant of God's children is indeed significant when he becomes himself a creative force, enters into God's work, and goes about his Father's business. What are the conquests of religion? Invariably you find that they are not the results of logic or demonstration; they have not come from crusades or other organizations: they are wrought by the flash which we like to call electric, from one devout, and loving, and hopeful life to another. As we felt a few days ago at an open grave, when we remembered how one woman's life had quickened and inspired other lives around her, while, perhaps, she had never taught a word of dogmatic, or never argued out a conclusion in language.

To live as an immortal means that one uses thus the things of earth and time for infinite results. The New Testament text on this matter is seldom understood, but covers the whole. The Saviour directs his disciples to use the things of this world in such wise that when they fail, as they must fail, the angels of light may receive them into everlasting habitations. It is as a boy of five years, on the carpet, may use his wooden blocks so as to take into the range of his knowledge those laws of gravitation on which the movements of planets and comets depend. It is to make my bargains at the grocer's shop with that courtesy, that integrity, that justice and steadiness with which I should talk with Raphael or Uriel if I happened to be in the business of Paradise Lost, and should show them that I was quite their equal in all matters of conscience and inspiration. Or, in a word, it is to bear in mind all along that, though the sun is to set to-night at five o'clock, there are regions of space where it never sets; and though the sun is burning itself out and will be done with when some myriads of æons of ages have gone by, that I, who walk in the shadow or in the sunlight, am never to be done with, and that I may use the shadow or the sunlight for my affair without any slavish subserviency to their accidental changes.

For training in this consciousness and certainty of infinite life I am, as you know, always urging young people to be familiar with the processes of nature, as one sees them where they are not controlled, — not harnessed for immediate and temporary purposes. Such a sleigh-ride as that of last week, in an hour of the glory of nature, lifts a man above mere earthy entanglements, as no logical demonstration of his being can do, and as very little formal poetry does. Whenever Scripture achieves such a miracle, wherever we find that Scripture, it is then that we call it inspired. For inspiration is the presence of the Infinite or Holy Spirit in words, in inventions, in heroism, or in any other human affair. Whether, then, one study nature through the revelations of the microscope, whether he study nature in the stars at night, whether he study nature as he opens a bud to see how life is enlarging itself and preparing to enlarge itself, or whether he study the old records of the folding of the strata into mountains, or travel afar, afoot or on the seas, that he may know more, whether of the curve of waves or the heaving up of sands, he trains himself to infinite life all the time. One does not say to "larger" life, because that word is too small, but to a life which is infinite, unbounded, and does not know our measure of great or little. Every step that the schools make in this direction is a gain in real education, whether it be or be not an advance in instruction. The use of the Natural History Society, of the museums, of such clubs as the Appalachian Club, and everything which calls men out from their handicrafts, whether of the brain or of the fingers, into this sympathy with the life of the world and of the universe, is so much help to him who is thus emancipated. Indeed, I suppose that here is the real reason why, at bottom and at heart, imprisonment, or being shut up away from the courses of nature, has come to be rightly esteemed as the most terrible punishment which man can inflict upon his brother. The man who eagerly and continuously tries in such fashion to cultivate the infinite secret of nature lives as an immortal.

It is virtually to say the same thing, — simply with a change of the illustration, — when one speaks of that enlargement of life as infinite which comes from frankly throwing ourselves into the great brotherhood of mankind. Of course I may go about my daily business merely with the wish to make a profit for myself, — to receive more than I give out, to be richer to-night than I was this morning. But I may go into it with the enthusiasm with which a great general makes an army move because he loves his country. Every thread in my shuttle as I throw it across the loom, every word that I write upon the paper, or every type which I set in my composing-stick, may be my contribution to the welfare of mankind. I heard a man say once that he had rather live in a work-shop than in a trade-shop. What he meant was that he wanted to be a contributor to the real comfort of the whole human race. He liked to feel, when he made a screw, that that screw was of use in South Africa or in Alaska. He liked to feel that he was doing his part as a creative force, and that God had not miscalculated when He sent him into the world. I see no reason why a man in a trade-shop should not have the same feeling; but perhaps it does not suggest itself quite so readily. Trade-shop or work-shop, wherever a man is, if he be at work in the brotherhood, and bears in mind the service he is rendering for the brotherhood, he will be lifted wholly above the plane of the brute, eating that his own hunger may be appeased, and seeking forage that he may eat, and going and coming only that he may seek forage. In such service, as George Herbert says, there is nothing mean; in such service for mankind one comes, as in the study of nature, into the infinite relations. And as a thousand poets have sung and a thousand philosophers have said, this service also extends itself beyond the range of 1892 or of this century. I touch the button today, but the thrill which results from my determination is a thrill which spreads not only through all space, but through all time. So far I am one with God and nature in the affair of His eternity.

"Blessed are the merciful, for they shall obtain mercy." This was the beatitude as the Saviour announced it on the mountain. To his own mind it involved the enlargement of merciful life of him who rendered this service or that service. He saw the disciple who had accepted the promise more and more godlike, more and more divine, a partner indeed of the universe, in precise proportion as he passed outside his own physical effort or enjoyment into the service which God, without leaving it Himself, had intrusted to His children of mankind.

To make one's life as large as this in its relations is to live as an immortal.

It is his business to enter into the life of the universe, his business to enter into the common life of his race, — yes, and to make it better. And whatever he does in such matters he does it under infinite law. He does not need to inquire what are the customs or statutes of people round him. His tenure is not a temporary tenure, and his laws are the eternal laws. Among the most interesting of the fairy tales of our time, or of classical times, are stories to illustrate such life. The gods descend to live with men, as Apollo with Admetus, as Jupiter with Deucalion and Pyrrha. The god so housed in a cabin by the hour must be indifferent to its discomforts. He must eat his bran bread as if it were ambrosia, and drink his black broth as if it were nectar. He must correct the errors of the housekeeping or of the farm as if he were setting right the movement of a planet. But he must not be critical about the bed in which he sleeps, or the grammar of those to whom he is talking. He is above such trifles, because he is divine; he is Jove, or the son of Jove; he is infinite, immortal.

Such stories owe their interest to our reminiscences of our own immortality and the sense of our infinity which they quicken in us. We are in these cabins of ours, or houses, or palaces — this house of our earthly tabernacle — for a few score years, — what matter whether twoscore, threescore, or four. No matter, if while I live them through I am speaking the old language of heaven, and do not lose my accent; doing the old work of heaven, though it be in the ploughing of a furrow or the amusement of a child, — if, indeed, I be not warped aside to the gluttony of a beast or the laziness of an oyster, but if I go about my Father's business.

Eye hath not seen, no, nor ear heard, no, nor hath it entered into the heart of man to imagine what are the infinite things open to those who love God. But God has revealed them by His Spirit. Whoso really liveth, — says the Saviour, making the same statement, — whoso liveth in the infinite life, whoso believeth that God is Father and that we are children, — he does not die. He shall never die. It is not to the argument of a logician that He intrusts this truth. He intrusts it to the infinite experience of a living man — a man who really lives; who lives and moves and has his being in his God.

IMITATORS OF GOD.

"Be ye imitators of God, as beloved children, and walk in love, as Christ also loved you."
EPHESIANS V. I.

IT is a bold demand. But absolute religion is satisfied with nothing less. As we open a new year, it is the demand we are to keep in sight. These plans of ours are not the plans of beasts or of fishes or insects. They are the plans of children of God. We propose to enter that infinite life in 1892. We propose to discover that land of our bounded range which, perhaps, we have never seen before. We are of God's nature. We propose to do His will. We will be imitators of God.

A boy changes into a man when he takes his instructions from headquarters,—when he asks God what is his duty to-day, and from Him takes his answer.

It is thus, also, that a girl changes into a woman. The change in women comes more suddenly than with men. You leave your little girl playmate for three months, and when you meet her after that time you find she is another person. A greater change comes over her in that time than comes over a boy in many years.

Boys, on the other hand, are much more apt than girls to be separated from home early in life. They have to form the habit then of going to headquarters, and many a man will tell you that his seriousness of life, his consecration to life, began when he made the change from his early home.

Our business to-day is to ask carefully what help, if any, can be given to boy or girl in this business. How shall a man so order his life that he may have every day the personal intimacy with God which will, *first*, tell him what he has to do, and, *second*, give him the strength and judgment with which to do it, in his imitation of God.

I make it a rule of my own life to see every day some one whom I know to be my superior. But it is very difficult to enforce this rule. Often and often I fail, — I am always sorry when I fail, — but one cannot command events. The man or woman you want to see may not be at home; or, in the fifteen minutes you have for the interview, you may be waiting for a street-car at the corner. You and I must not complain when our plans break down — if we have done our part. That probably means that the plans of One who knows more than we do have succeeded. But if you and I find this difficulty in intimacies with personal friends here, it is our business to care even more assiduously about our daily conversation and intimacy with the nearest of our friends, the most powerful and the most loving, and to be sure that there, at least, no circumstance or accident of time or of place shall prevent the interview.

Young men or women will be really in earnest about this if they have fairly tried the great experiment themselves, or if they have rightly and carefully ordered life, in the recognition of Our Father as a personal friend, seeking His advice, and acting by it.

Take the Life of lives, the life of the Leader of leaders, the Lord of lords, the Saviour of men. We begin to see as mere matter of fact and outside history how he is becoming King of kings for this world. Of that life, the centre is daily communion with God. He sets on foot the great practical movement which changed the world. He sends out two and two, his twelve apostles, — yes, and he does this after spending the night in prayer. He had gone away to the mountain solitude that he might tell his Father what he needed, and from his Father receive directions.

Read Paul with any attention, and you find the same thing. All that is said there about the Spirit explaining this, and the Spirit explaining that, — about the apostles receiving this from the Spirit and that from the Spirit, — means simply that he did not trust only to any logic of his own, or any observation of his own, but that he sought the Holy Spirit, whose other name is Our Father.

Bear in mind all along that any distinction between Our Father and the present Holy Spirit is merely artificial and technical, and the folly of the schools. I must not take time about this, but the same truth holds all through history. The moment you come upon any one of the world's real leaders — there are not many of them — you come upon a man who was in distinct personal communion with God. The two instances which are perhaps most cited are very good ones. They are in the lives of Luther and Columbus, — two men who habitually retired from personal conversation with princes, and captains, and other men, that they might ask God what their duty was, and from Him might receive, first, an answer to that question, and, second, the power by which they were to discharge that duty. Mr. Fiske has just now made the statement — which for myself I think will be received very seriously — that the first of living men, in the catalogue of men so far known, is Oliver Cromwell, the great founder of the English Commonwealth, the person to whose tenderness and wisdom we owe it that New England is New England. Determine this as you please, there is another instance where the power of the man comes from this daily communion with the infinite power which rules all worlds.

Simply stated, here is the law. The voice of that infinite power whom the Saviour called Our Father is what we call right, and the man who seeks his instructions at headquarters — if I may use the same figure I used before — is the person who succeeds in doing right; and the person who does right has the alliance of angels and archangels, and of all good men and women.

This I say as a simple outside fact of history, which must attract the attention of any intelligent young man or young woman. Now, our business to-day is to ask whether there are any methods or forms which can assist the young man or young woman who has highly resolved in every day to hold this personal communion with the All-Father, Our Father, the Infinite Spirit, whose voice is right? To help in this personal intimacy, these churches are formed. Let the leaders of them, and the members of them, hold well in mind that this is their central business. It will be a very good thing if our New Year's resolutions help to sustain the " Church of the Holy Spirit," or the " Sixth Congregational Church" of the town, or if it engage in active charities, or if the members become better acquainted with each other. All these are very good things, but our central business is to encourage young people to hold daily communion with God. That is what the church is, in the first place, for. They can try their wings in different ways, but the first business is to encourage them in learning to fly. And there is a certain danger, which we have all of us observed, that the interest of studying out the duties which will belong to him who has learned to fly, shall be so great that the other study of flight itself, of flying strongly and well, of mounting up on wings as eagles, shall slip out of sight and attention.

I have found no wiser rule, in the advice which I have given to young people, than that which I myself received from John Weiss. He said it in a sermon which he preached to the Unitarian convention at Portland, I suppose thirty years ago. To those doctors of divinity, men of learning, men of practice, manufacturers, merchants, inventors, to the mothers of families, to young men starting in life, to young women starting in life, he said, " Go away every day from other people, without their knowing it, and for five minutes or for ten minutes sit in a room by yourself to see if God has anything to say to you." I believe that to be an excellent, practical, four-square rule in the direction of life.

Side by side with this advice I tell young people who ask me for advice, to have in that room two or three of the books which they have found most helpful in this affair, or which their friends have found so. Here, in the first place, is the use of the Bible. It is not simply as a book of ethics that the Bible is valuable, certainly not as a book of history, least of all as a book of doctrine. Its value comes from its recording so much of the intimacy of men and women who have known how to live with Him who is the Author of life. And you do get expressions in the Psalms, the prophets, the Gospels, in the epistles, and in the Book of Revelation, which make real to you the absolute possible intimacy of the child with the Father, as hardly anything else in literature does. The Bible is therefore the prayer-book of Christians. When people talk to me of this or that liturgy with enthusiasm, I always try to listen civilly; but I always say, "There is no such book of prayers as the Bible." On this Bible you will put one or two of the books, from a small list,—I should not say more than ten or twelve,—which are easily accessible in the English language. A first-rate hymn book is one of these; and occasionally some one edits a collection of sacred poetry which is worth having there. Besides these, take your choice from Thomas à Kempis, which, if you can, you had better read in Latin; Fénelon, William Law, and Scougal. "Owen Feltham's Resolves" is a good book. So is The Roman Breviary, if you can read it in Latin; and for many reasons, Marcus Aurelius and Epictetus. I mention these because they are my favorites. Any good adviser will add three or four more of his favorites to the list. Observe, I do not mean that you shall have them all there at one time. But I would have some one or two of them beside the Bible. I would then cultivate the habit of going away, as Mr. Weiss says, to listen if God has anything to say to me. I would not hesitate to open at random into one, two, or three of these books, and take the particular suggestion which came to me and read a few lines. I would turn it over in my mind. But I would remember all along that this is not a mere intellectual process that I am engaged in. I am engaged in communion with the Infinite Spirit from which I am born, to which I return, whose work I share, whose light I can receive, and into whose joy I mean to enter.

So much for my personal duty. Now, so far as my influence goes in the household in which I live, I would unite this personal duty with the habit of the people in that house, or with those to whom I am closest bound, say my brothers and sisters, or my children. If, without any formality, or with as little as is possible, we can meet by the piano and sing a hymn every day, in the morning or in the evening, as may be most convenient, or if some one reads to us three or four verses of the Bible, or if we join together in saying the Lord's Prayer, or in reading from any other book of devotion, there is no question that we shall give ourselves a chance to go to that day's business, or the next day's business, more alive to the sense of the common life. We shall understand better that no one of us is paddling a separate boat, we shall see better that we are all engaged in one great enterprise, in one great voyage, and that in that voyage we have the power, and, as I said, the joy, if we want to take it, of Him who provides the life of each and all.

But both these endeavors — the endeavors for personal communion with God and the endeavor to quicken the whole circle of friends to a life nothing less than that of God's sons and daughters — involve our Sunday privilege in this place. When we meet each other in the street, in the cars, or at a party, we who see each other here on Sunday, we always have, as the central thought, the place where we met last, and the dominant of this church and this hour of song and prayer. We, at least, need not begin with talk about the weather. We have met God in each other's company. We are at home in His house together, and so far we are at home with each other wherever we go. So we have for such upward flight as I have described, the great help of the sympathy of "Together."

And thus what I have said leads us to speak of public worship. For the endeavors for personal communion and any step toward quickening the circle in which we live, — all suggest a wider intimacy. If, when one of us goes into another house to visit, this custom of singing a hymn together at the piano is a custom which has been taken up in all the houses in the town, there will be less of what I call formality about it. It will not seem a matter of mechanism, it will seem a simple matter of the regular daily life. We shall accept it as we accept the fact that every family takes a newspaper. It will not seem any more strange. And that analogy might be pushed: one family takes one newspaper and another takes another. So, these different families might signify their accord in worship of the life of God in different ways; but is not it clear enough, that some such general organization with this object as every Sunday enforces will help every separate household in the wish and effort to draw closer to God as every day goes by?

To repeat words which I heard last week by a real leader of men, what we want in New England is to encourage usages of piety. There is no reason to think that there is less piety now than there ever was — that is, less love of God. What is desirable is that the usages of piety shall be kept even with the other usages of the time, and that in the crowd and pressure of our daily life these usages shall not be thrust out of sight, out of hearing, or out of the memory.

Now it is for this very thing that the church gathers us here every Sunday for this winter. It is for this that the noblest genius composes for us the sacred music of the Mass. For this that we do our best to interpret it. For this that we ask these children to meet in the Sunday-school. For this, really, that the great machine of public instruction is desired. For this that the Public

Library asks you to turn aside from chatter and commune with the noblest men and the best women. And this is the promise. If to-day, which is happily shielded from the clatter and hurry of yesterday: if you will so far set in order in an hour's careful resolution, your half-formed plans for the winter, so that beyond peradventure the Spirit of God shall give to all life, and the dignity of life; if, I do not say in an hour's resolution, but in the prayer of one minute, you gain God's confirmation of such a purpose, you shall know this day twelvemonth, as none of my parables can teach you, what Paul meant when he said, "Walk in the Spirit," and what Christ meant when he said, "Life more abundantly." You shall quit the little stagnant pool of the dock in which your ship has laid since she was built, and you shall sail fresh and free over the unending ocean. We have all the same power of eyesight. But an East Indian fakir bends his head downward and uses his eyesight always to contemplate the heart-beat in his own bosom. He calls that "consecration." Another trains His eyes and fortifies them to look through the heavens, with this or that enginery of the observatory, so that he shall walk with Orion in his courses, and be a freeman of the universe, with the privileges of Arcturus and his suns. The one of them has the same optic nerve as the other. But the range, the life, are so far different. The body is earthly. Care for it; attend to it, — and so far your life is earthly too. Its heavenly side is the outside. It extends as far as the universe extends; as far as the God who rules that universe. Make Him your daily companion; talk to Him; listen to Him; walk with Him; work with Him; — and you find what is the abundance of Life. You find the meaning of that phrase, "The kingdom of God." You have the certainty of the present heaven.

[This sermon was preached as a New Year's sermon at the South Congregational Church.]

INSTALLATION OF REV. JOHN CUCKSON.

ARLINGTON-STREET CHURCH, BOSTON, MAY 11, 1892.

We also, when we were children, were held in bondage, — but when the fulness of time came, God sent forth his Son that we might receive the adoption of sons.

GALATIANS iv. 3, 4.

IT is impossible to meet here, with the happy outlook of this occasion, without recalling the memories of this pulpit, and of that famous church in Federal street from which so much went forth for the blessing of the world.

Its modern history begins when Jeremiah Belknap, with his own wisdom and devotion, led it out from the somewhat limited notions of a circle of Scotch exiles, singing the songs of the Lord in a strange land. We owe to him a great step forward in the selection of our hymns. I think his hymn-book is not now in use, but I have used it in public service. Will you let me indulge myself, as we install a new minister in this honored pulpit, by saying just a word of each of his four last predecessors? Each of them honored me with his personal friendship.

Edward E. Hale.

The amazed critics of his own time generally tried to account for Channing's power, by tracing out the clearness and directness of his thought, as if his were to be counted as intellectual victories. But they were quite wrong. Here was a child of God, — who had found out that he was a child of God, and delighted in the relationship. Channing was a mystic, through and through, — using that word in its proper sense, of one who is possessed by the Infinite Spirit, and trusts himself to the inspiration. The eager hopes and prayers, especially of the early years of his biography, are to be remembered with any of those most prized among the most devout saints, as A Kempis, or Molinos, or Scougal, or the Wesleys. And here was the real power which moved this century. Omnipotence is apt to move that with which it has to do. It is interesting to see that men did not make this real to themselves until, after his death, his biography was published. Then from his own private notes they could see his eagerness to accept the life of God as his life, and his only life. So resolute is the human passion for ascribing power to method, or to machinery, instead of looking to the Author of Being and Fountain of Life, that the earlier critics of Channing preferred to speak of him as an intellectual wonder.

To be the coadjutor and helper of such a saint came the young Gannett, who honored and loved him. With absolute self-renunciation, he was only eager to do in this church what it was convenient for Dr. Channing not to do. That Dr. Channing might be well and able to do his part, and that Satan might be beaten wherever he showed his head, — this was the double purpose to which this young man consecrated his daily life. And he took care to make himself of no reputation as he took that double duty. I remember so well how with his quick step and firm, erect carriage, hair black as the raven, and words rapid and sharp, he would enter any of our pulpits, and how he controlled his hearers! Certainly we boys wanted nothing better than we heard from him, even in the beginning.

And his work afterwards — I do not speak of this church only, but for the Unitarian church of New England, which he led — was that of enlivenment. He knew no such word as "fail" in those days. He accepted for the Unitarian church the moral and intellectual leadership which in those days people were not unwilling to give it. He had the great advantage, for that position, of a fixed and definite theology, — of which he was as sure as an astronomer is of the law of the attraction of gravitation. To see any of the youngsters fall away from this was terrible to him, but never did he doubt that truth is truth and must prevail.

Of Mr. Ware — with our fresh memories of his

life, and of what seemed a death too early — it is harder to speak in this presence. Those who only knew him in the years — all too few — of his work in this church, know one who was carrying on a daily martyr struggle against concealed disease, so manfully, that people would speak to him as if he were in high health, when he was suffering as by no chance he would say. But we, who had known him from boyhood, like to think of those earlier days of vigor; of his visits to the army, in the field or in the camp; of his large view of the situation there, and of the duty of the church behind the army. His call to those at home, to do their duty to those under canvas or in the entrenchments, was a clarion cry. And it would be safe and fair to say that to Henry Bellows, Charles Lowe, and John Ware, more than to any other of our preachers, did the Unitarian church owe the new sense of its lead, of the central dignity of its position in national life, which culminated in the organization of our National Conference. It is hardly to be spoken of as a coincidence, it was rather the record of a necessary connection of time, that the first authoritative convention of the united Unitarian church of America was held in New York, on the same day when Richmond surrendered to the Union army.

And of our dear friend Herford, who has left us now to take up harder duty in England, — with our fresh memories of his cordial love, —

there is no need to speak. Fit workman indeed was he, in a field where such noble workmen had gone before him. And the living force of this church to-day, and its vigorous equipment of men, women, and means for worship, for charity, for education, and for hospitality, make a token which all men understand, of the efficiency and spirit which he consecrated to the work of this church, and to no work beside. What this church ought to do in the largest interpretation of its service, — what the Unitarian church of America ought to do, — to that he would give every throb of his pulse, every thought, every act, every minute. For any other duty or exigency, no! Here was his place and opportunity. And we know how large he made his place and how noble his opportunity.

It is worth while merely to call together such memories of four lives so different in their method, but all so intensely alive. It is worth while, because our business to-night is to look back on those lessons which this church has learned and taught, so that we may translate their lessons into the language, yes, and the purposes, of this half-century before us. Of that half-century you younger men and women must highly resolve to-night that you will be among the spiritual, and so the moral, leaders. If we are to take in at one view seventy or eighty years, I could hardly name any one church in Christendom where, Sunday after Sunday, men have taken such a view as has been taken here of the present advance of the Idea — of the victory of the Spirit. Dr. Channing's hearers were thinking of one line of advance; in a way, Dr. Gannett's were thinking of another; Mr. Ware's had yet another picture before them; and Dr. Herford spoke — of course he spoke — in an atmosphere different once more. But this church, in those eighty years, has never had a minister which told it that it had "entered into its rest." Nobody ever stood here to tell this congregation that they were to forget the things that are before, while they reached back to those things that are behind. That is the duty, alas! of some churches, or they are told so; but not of the church in Federal street or in Arlington street. And that which is incumbent, of course, in every installation festival is specially agreeable here, because specially hopeful. It is always pleasant to prophesy when there is so good a chance that prophecy will come true.

It is seventy-three years last Thursday since, at Baltimore, Mr. Channing, then only thirty-nine years old, preached the celebrated sermon, well remembered, which distinctly announced to the American church that the little company of organized Unitarians had a mission which it meant to perform. Up till that time most people, even religious people, had persuaded themselves that the truth might be left to overcome error within the church, gradually and without conflict. People tried to think that old fables would die of themselves if they were only let alone; and that all this was so certain that no one need make a fuss about it. But at the Baltimore dedication Mr. Channing blew the bugle of attack. Or that would be a better figure which said, that this quiet champion, in the presence of a curious company of people, who wondered what this old-new doctrine, or new-old doctrine, was, walked quietly through the ancient, dignified temple of Calvinism, and there, in the presence of decorous priests who hoped the thing would outlast their time, struck in the face every one of the idols, on the right hand and on the left hand, as he passed them by. It was not contempt any longer. It was not silence any longer. It was square attack — attack all along the line. What was worse, he justified what he had done, in statement and logic which no one could overthrow.

Seventy-three years have passed since then. The idols still exist, perhaps. I have been told that some of them can be found in museums. Perhaps it is so. I do not know. I do know that no one worships them. I know that there are no priests who like to be reminded of them. I know that the church of America, from the left wing to the right, has diligently and discreetly packed its Calvinism wholly out of the way. I think there are some written creeds which avow it; but in these days we are told that the creeds and articles of churches are of no consequence. I have even been told by the highest authority that their presence in books, once regarded as standards, is mere matter of the bookbinder!

Of New England I know more. I am fond of repeating the story — which expresses the precise truth — of what Dean Stanley said, when he returned to England from his visit here. "Of course," he said, "I went to hear them preach whenever I could, chiefly in the Evangelical churches. Many men I heard in many pulpits of different names, but the preacher was always Ralph Waldo Emerson." No man can observe the working theology of our time without seeing that our great idealist of this century is everywhere the leader. And no one notes wisely the movement in any church who does not see that it is an aggressive movement, seeking to build up the Kingdom of God.

True, there are men who would tell you, as they would have told you a hundred years ago, that the chief business of the pulpit is in its appeal to separate hearers, for the saving of their separate souls. But even these men would say that they want to save the soul of the separate hearer so that that hearer may go to work as an apostle, to bring in the Kingdom of God. They may cry, "Repent ye!" but like John the Baptist they cry, "Repent ye, because the Kingdom of God is at hand!" That God is the present ruler, that God is immanent in all life, — this is the religious doctrine of our time. From east to west, — from the right wing to the left wing, — from the pulpit of the Church of Rome to the exhortation of a Quaker conference, this is the statement and appeal. In such an outlook as we are attempting now; in your reconsecration of yourselves to-night as a church of Christ; in the reconsecration of this man to the ministry of Christ, — the dominant question is: How can these eternal truths best be brought into the impending movement of the next century? How are we to lift men, in the terrible wealth and prosperity which belongs to their physical successes? How are we to lift them away from the temptations of dust and mud and smoke, into the infinite life of the sons of God?

It is clear enough that it is a game of giants which we look forward to. The man who had only his hand to fight with, has a club to swing in the future. The conspirator who had to be satisfied with words, finds now that he can make dynamite in his kitchen. The workman who was glad to work twelve hours, is able to make his own terms for eight. This is simply to say that man has now a hundred times the power for good or for evil that he had sixty years ago. If, as we here all suppose, this power can be controlled by laws; if it is to be, as on the whole it always has been, swayed by moral agencies, — its increase is simply a benediction, and is one more step forward and upward of the world. But all the more have those who lead the world, or who mean to, to find how the moral forces are to be used, where they come from, and how they shall be proclaimed.

This may be said, as the basis of all our answers, that church and pulpit have given up everywhere the attitude of defiance. No pulpit threatens anybody now. Hell may be kept in the creed; but in appeal it is wisely left in the background. On the other hand, in all communions the appeal is made to man's affections, to his hopes, and more and more to his judgment.

This is the more important because none of the great floods of enthusiasm in history which have successfully united men and compelled them to move together have been swayed by men's terrors. Peter the Hermit roused all Europe to march to recover the Holy Sepulchre, by telling Europe how unjustly the Christians were treated on the very spot where the Master died. He did not alarm his hearers. John Gough, Hawkins, and the other Washingtonian leaders in 1840 compelled men to tread under foot the temptation of liquor, and combined them in a common cause by showing to them that they might be leaders where they were slaves, and begging them to work to lift others from their ruin. The great uprising of the North, in 1861, was anything but a spasm of fear. Nor was it, in the outset, a determination to end slavery. It was the determination even higher, to assert the majesty of the nation. The real rulers of the nation had, generally, from the time when it was formed, left the rule of it to the Southern oligarchy, which was, as it is, willing enough to take in hand that care. But that oligarchy at last stepped too far, and the giant woke. The people asserted its place, and the pretender was, for twenty years, nowhere. In all these cases, the appeal of the leaders was to the nobler sentiments of the rank and file, and not to their fears of hunger, of pain, or of other penalty.

Now the question for you who have the next half-century to direct is what the form of appeal shall be by which you shall embody power which is clearly matchless, if only you can win it on your side.

The Saviour of men, coming into social conditions wholly different, begged men, advised them, commanded them, to turn from all other theories of life and to proclaim the law of God as the present law of village, city, home, synagogue, court, and camp. "Go and preach the Kingdom of God," he said, "and preach it all over this world." That voice's echo has not died. Your question in the business you have in hand, for these fifty years, is to find out how that appeal can be made to most purpose now, and then to make it with all your might day by day on those lines.

In that business we have a good analogy, and I should say a fair working example, in the most remarkable single element of our national strength. I mean the absolute loyalty of the separate citizen to the country, — unless he be wholly spoiled by inherited wealth, — and his certainty of her power and success. The earlier travellers from Europe all noticed this, and it enraged them. You toiled over execrable roads for a day, travelling through a wilderness. At night you slept in a dirty cabin, the guest of a man who could hardly speak his own language. This man was using an axe which was made in England; he carried a gun which was made in England; his very ploughshare and hoe were made in England; and yet, infallibly, he told his tired and annoyed guest that America was yet to "whip every nation in the world," — that she was to go beyond them all in civilization, and art, and invention. When he was asked to compare his squalid cabin with the home which for some reason his guest had left, he said he did not care for that contrast; that America would be the greatest nation in the world, that he knew it, and that his guest had only to wait a little and he would know it too.

This intense arrogance, naturally enough, was wholly unintelligible to people who came from feudal countries. Certainly they had never seen it at home. No peasant in England, or France, or Germany spoke with any such prophetic intimation. And there was something maddening to a man who had, for some reason, left all the luxuries of civilization behind him, to be told that all these were really of no account, compared with the glories which were about to dawn on the cabin in which he was half starved, and on the wilderness through which he was yet to travel.

But, to look on the other side, there is something really sublime in this arrogance, when one observes its source. For the first time in the world's history, such men as this braggart savage had been admitted to every privilege of humanity. He had been told to hew his own way, to build his own house, to live his own life. Feudal customs, feudal religion among the rest, had always, till now, bidden him do his duty in that condition of life in which God had placed him. Yes; and feudal customs had bound him to that condition very tightly. Now this new nation bade him "go as he pleased." True, she gave him nothing to go with. That was his affair. But, on the other hand, if she gave no cross of honor to any Athelstan, she had no manacle for any Wamba. Fool or baron, they were all one to her. Let each man live his own life, and make his own career, she said. Now it was a native instinct of gratitude which compelled each such Wamba, the son of Witless, each man so blessed and gifted, to praise the mother who had so blessed him. And it was an instinct which has proved true, by which he foretold the unanimous service to her of her sons. As it has proved, the material wealth of this nation does not rest primarily in her mines or in her crops. It is in that system of open promotion, by which that man is sure to come to the front who knows how to smelt the mineral, or to reap the harvest, and is industrious enough to do so.

Now, one has nothing but laughter for the arrogant boast of the half-clad frontiersman. But one does see at the same time what unsubsidized power the nation has won, when, by her fundamental system, she controls and commands, yes, to the very last throb and drop, the united forces of every such man within her borders.

Take that little analogy now, and carry it to the range and field vastly higher and larger, with which we are concerned, in our problem here: How we shall lead the next half-century. We have abandoned the narrow ground with which the old church was satisfied. We, too, in the Liberal communions, have announced, and shall announce, to all men that they are nothing less than the sons of God; to all women, that they are his daughters. The older church, almost with a droll grimace, reserving for salvation and eternal blessing all her ordained clergy, bade them tell all the rest of mankind that *they* were born in sin and conceived in iniquity, and that nine-tenths of them would certainly be damned in eternal torment. All the more, she said, must the other tenth turn and live, and proclaim to the nine-tenths, and to each other, the present love of a present God, and his present kingdom. But can we wonder if the answer to that demand was variable and fluttering? Is it strange that when men heard such an invitation, one turned to his farm and another to his merchandise? Had the church, in a word, any right to expect much enthusiasm in the world's reply?

No. But let the teachers of the world take up in good faith, and to the outer end, the Saviour's appeal and direction. Let them go into the highways and the byways. Let them call the vinedresser, and the harlot, and the publican. Let them say, " Ye are all kings and all priests," believing it themselves. Let them say to the publican, " God makes this demand upon you; " and to the harlot, " God makes this demand upon you." The century which dares make that demand has a right, which no other century has deserved, to an enthusiastic reply. It has myriads to call *en masse*, where the old theologians were recruiting here and there a man who could be tempted by a ribbon or a shilling. And it is likely to learn, as no century has learned before, what the Master of Men meant, when, to a flock where every sheep and every lamb tried to do his duty, he said in such solemn prophecy: "Your Father shall give you the kingdom."

That religion belongs to all sorts and conditions of men, — to sinner as well as saint, to blackleg as well as gentleman, — that is our gospel. The decorous selection of a clergy with the great name "the church," as if the rest must not share in sacraments, must not understand theology, nay, need not believe in creeds, — this is to be done with forever. God has work to do; they are all to be taught this. You can do it. They are to be thus encouraged. You must do it. They are to be thus warned. And every mother's son of us has the right to warn them, as, if the village were in flames at night, every man who is awake has a right to cry, "Fire!" We are not rallying for our philanthropies or our educations only those who know where sin came from, or those who can explain evolution. It is not the theologians only whom we are to enlist. It is the sons and daughters of God; it is every one who draws a breath of his air or who lives in his sunshine, who is to listen for his word and to bring in his kingdom. And they are, each and all, to understand that the coming of the kingdom depends not only upon Him, but upon them as much and as well.

The work is thus to be done by the whole family of God. It is not left to any selected hierarchy, not left to the work of any remnant, designated by some apostolic succession. To every one we may appeal, expecting from every one some assistance.

This is the first characteristic of the religious appeal of the next half-century; and with it, of course, belongs first, second, last, and always, the statement, perfectly familiar in the first century, but new in the nineteenth, that God is on our side. Nature is with us and not against us. The power that rules the universe loves us and does not hate us. We need no longer speak of the church as the huddled fragment floating on the logs of a drifting raft where the world has perished. We speak to those who are born of God and to God return, who live in his life, love with his love, rest in his arms, tell him everything, and receive everything from a Father's perfect tenderness. Do we tell them that they are fellow-workers with God? We tell them as well that God is a fellow-worker with them. Perhaps it is in this appeal, more than in any other which we have to make, by which we surprise those who have been awe-struck, I might say paralyzed, under the pressure of mediæval theologies. But whether men take it simply or with surprise, we are thus to appeal always. As Mr. Brown said so well, "We teach them the humanity of God while we teach them the divinity of man." We teach them that in those processes which we call the processes of present Nature, as well as in work of His, long ages ago, there is the present love of a Holy Spirit, which is ready to inspire the baby in his play, the smith at his anvil, the speaker in the forum, the nurse at the bedside, or the seaman on the ocean. God is with us, and we are with him.

Our Hungarian friends, with their own fire and pathos, told me the story of their first victory, centuries ago, in Kolosvar. Their great prophet of the North, who did not even speak their wonderful Magyar language well, appealed to them as the children of the living God. He gave them some sense — alas, no man wrote down the words! — of what it is to come to God in your own prayer, with no priest between; of what it is to trust in the infinite strength, and in no transfer of power to machinery. Speaking with God's voice himself, he spoke to God's children of God's present power. And they, on the moment, with a storm of passionate conviction, lifted him in their arms from the stone, which they still show, where he was addressing them. They carried him into the cathedral of their city; and to frightened priests, looking back to some old records for their information, they cried out that they had here a prophet of the living God, who was to speak now the eternal truth. Priests of an apostolic succession and machinery of worship vanished at the cry, from the place, and were gone for centuries. It became a place which should proclaim the fatherhood of God and the brotherhood of man.

One does not wonder at such a miracle when one remembers the power by which it was effected.

We have much the same miracle to work to-day, — not in driving out priests from their sanctuaries, but in bringing the sense of God into the workshop and school and cabin; into the mining of silver, and the weaving of cotton, and the carrying of corn. The immanent presence of the living God, — is this the gospel which we are to preach? Yes; and it is as well the power by which we are to proclaim that gospel. And we need ask few questions as to method or organization, when that Spirit sends us forth, conquering and to conquer.

As I see the forward look with which men regard the new century, it seems to me that all their drift is hopeful. The fixed habit of men, of all sorts and conditions, seems to me to be hope, and not despair. "You will be wise," I heard a great man of finance say, "if in your investments you bet on the country." It seems to me that I see the same disposition to "bet on the world;" that men look forward cheerfully, and look backward less. Every scheme of social reform, though it seem to me absurd, and may be absurd, means that men are determined that the Kingdom shall come. They may not put it in those words, but that is their hope and their purpose. Digging their long trench in Sinaloa; publishing their new plans of social order in New York or Chicago; studying their Bellamy, or writing new ones which they think better, — everywhere the magic of hope stays up the life, which would have been abject and powerless were it left to despair. To direct, as to encourage such hope, and to lead such enterprise, is the special business of the people like you, who have, with your eyes open, accepted and professed a religion of hope, in the place and on the ruins of a theology of darkness. It is ours to see that such plans shall not be absurd, that such prophecies shall not disappoint themselves. This we can only do, as we live ourselves in actual communion with a loving God, — as for ourselves we determine that we will not live, — live with him, for ourselves alone, and as with him and for other men — we make these homes and workshops of ours to be a present heaven.

We consecrate ourselves anew to-night with such high determination. Gladly we intrust this church, with its noble history, to such ministry for another century — of faith and hope and love. Its new ministry asks no better omens than its history affords. A church which definitely and distinctly proclaims its determination to follow where this present Holy Spirit leads, need ask for no inferior ally.

DO YOU READ
LEND A HAND?

It is a Monthly Magazine of the First Class.

EDWARD E. HALE, D.D.,
Editor-in-Chief.

It deals with charities and reforms, and gives hints to all philanthropic workers. Reports of the Ramabai Association may be found each month in its pages. Indian Associations are ably represented among its contributors.

It condenses the reports of all the leading charitable societies, so that a set of LEND A HAND is a record of progress in Social Reform for the last few years.

Its circulation is national, extending to all parts of the country, and the wide circle of its regular contributors secures information and description of plans for improvement in all parts of America.

PRICE, $2.00 A YEAR.

J. STILMAN SMITH & CO., Publishers.

THE FOLLOWING BOOKS
By EDWARD E. HALE

will be sent on receipt of price.

IN HIS NAME, ...	$1.00, pap., 25 cents.
TEN TIMES ONE IS TEN, . .	$1.00, pap., 25 cents.
THE MALTESE CROSS. A Story, . . .	10 cents.
MAN WITHOUT A COUNTRY, ...	50 cents.
boards, 25 cents, pap., 20 cents.	
DAILY BREAD, ...	20 cents.
RED AND WHITE, ...	20 cents.
NEITHER SCRIP NOR MONEY, ...	20 cents.

Maltese Crosses for Badges, I. H. N. Charms or Pins. 25 cents each, $2.75 per dozen.

Coin Silver Charms or Pins, 40 cents each, $4.50 per doz.

Address,

J. STILMAN SMITH & CO.,

3 Hamilton Place, Boston.

A NEW SCHOOL READER.

Edward Everett Hale's Patriotic Story,

"THE MAN WITHOUT A COUNTRY."

This little book, written during the war, and intended to assist in raising the standard of love of country and true patriotism, is well fitted for the study of our young people to-day.

Its pure English and vivid descriptions, added to its patriotic character, make it eminently a fit book for supplementary reading in grammar and high schools.

Printed on white paper with clear type, and bound in attractive covers displaying the American flag, it cannot fail to please.

Cloth, 50 cents; board covers, 25 cents; paper covers, 20 cents.

Sent, postpaid, on receipt of price.

We are glad to send sample copies to superintendents or teachers of schools for 15 cents.

We make a liberal discount to schools.

J. STILMAN. SMITH & CO.,

Publishers,

3 Hamilton Place, Boston, Mass.

www.ingramcontent.com/pod-product-compliance
Lightning Source LLC
Chambersburg PA
CBHW031408160426
43196CB00007B/941